About this Guide

This guide is intended to provide an introduction to accepted best practice in the area of information security management. Corporate governance is now firmly on the agenda of all PLCs and the concept of good stewardship embedded in that structure requires Directors to understand and protect their company assets. It is widely accepted that corporate information, in the shape of patents, designs, licences and documents, forms an increasingly significant aspect of those company assets.

In the field of e-commerce, ISO17799—the International Standard for information security management—is becoming increasingly recognised as the accepted framework on which to base international best practice. The advice in this guide is presented at a level of detail aimed at those who either are new to the subject or would like to become more familiar with the scope of this subject and with the terms and expressions used in relation to it. For those who seek more in-depth detail, it is worth noting that the text of this new International Standards Organisation document ISO 17799 is based on the long-standing British Standard 7799 and reflects how the management concepts embedded in the earlier BSI text have been adopted as the *de facto* standard for information security management by many countries around the world.

The title *Information Security Management* was deliberately chosen to emphasise the need for this fundamental component of good business practice to be addressed as an aspect of general management rather than as a new and separate topic. It is clear that security is a matter of identifying valuable assets and deciding how best to safeguard them. It is equally clear that the art of making assets secure involves locks, bolts and bars, be they physical or logical devices. However, experience shows us that most breaches are not the result of locks failing to work. By far the greatest number of commercial security breaches are directly attributable to the failure of people to comply with the rules and objectives of their own security policies. Failures such as doors wedged open with fire extinguishers and passwords left written on desk-top pads are still the greatest threats to good security practice.

This guide is intended to provide a general introduction to the terminology and issues that senior managers must understand if they are to meet the ever-increasing needs to comply with the requirements of corporate governance. ISO 17799 is divided into ten complementary sections or clauses. As with most well laid out standards there is a degree of chronology to the layout, in that the first section deals with policy and the subsequent sections evolve from that. It is also significant that each of the ten sections is equally important as a component of good security management.

In brief, the ten steps to good security management are:

Step 1. **Security policy**: a top-level statement endorsed by the management team on which all security precautions are subsequently based.

Step 2. **Security organisation**: a published security organisation that shows clearly who is responsible for security and who is authorised to deal with security issues.

Step 3. **Assets, classification and control**: a good understanding of what is important to the company and where good security is important.

Step 4. **Personnel security**: careful recruiting of personnel employed in key positions.

Step 5. **Physical and environmental security**: ensuring that the physical security precautions match the need expressed in the corporate policy.

A   ꜞ

INFORMATION
SECURITY
MANAGEMENT

Brian Doswell and
David Lilburn Watson

Perpetuity Press Ltd
PO Box 376 Leicester LE2 1UP UK
Telephone: +44 (0) 116 221 7778
Fax: +44 (0) 116 221 7171

214 N. Houston
Comanche Texas 76442 USA
Telephone: +1 915 356 7048
Fax: +1 915 356 3093

Email: info@perpetuitypress.com
Website: http://www.perpetuitypress.com

First published 2002

British Library Cataloguing in Publication Data.
A catalogue record for this book is available from the British
Library.

A Guide to Information Security Management
by Brian Doswell and David Lilburn Watson

ISBN 1 899 287 60 4

Step 6. **Computer and network management**: the provision of adequate tools and services to ensure that corporate information in these systems is properly protected.

Step 7. **System access control**: close monitoring of and control over who is authorised to read and to amend company information, especially within the computer systems.

Step 8. **Systems development and maintenance**: the need to ensure that future developments continue to embody the strength of protection in subsequent generations of production services.

Step 9. **Business continuity management**: the ability to minimise the impact of major disasters on the business processes, and to provide comprehensive backup strategies to ensure that no corporate data is lost.

Step 10. **Compliance**: the need to ensure that once good controls are put in place they continue to work and to deliver the required level of protection to the company's asset.

Contents

Section 1   10 Key Questions   9

Section 2   E-commerce and Information Security   11
               Management

Section 3   Security Policy   19

Section 4   Security Organisation   23

Section 5   Assets, Classification and Control   27

Section 6   Personnel Security   31

Section 7   Physical and Environmental Security   35

Section 8   Computer and Network Management   39

Section 9   System Access Control   45

Section 10   Systems Development and Maintenance   51

Section 11   Business Continuity Planning   57

Section 12   Compliance   61

Section 1
10 Key Questions

Information security is a management issue that requires senior managers to understand and implement those best practice issues that form the basis of good corporate information security. If we accept that all companies are different and deliver their respective goods and services in different ways, how can one set of best-practice rules apply across the board?

The answer is that each company must understand and define its own need for information security. Having done that, the advice and guidance for implementing information security around those assets that the company has identified as being valuable, critical and important to their specific business remains essentially similar. There are no precise metrics for risk analysis. Each risk review will depend largely on the degree of vulnerability felt by the management team in place at the time, and the need to provide corresponding countermeasures will vary according to their views. Some companies may choose to accept and ignore the impact of risks that others are bound by their regulators or by statutory rule to manage. Whatever the case, it is important that a detailed risk analysis be completed in a way that can be demonstrated by the Board. In simple terms the Board must be able to answer these ten questions:

1.   Is information security management relevant to your business?

2.   Do you have a company information security policy?

3.   Who in your company management has the greatest impact on the management of information security?

4.   How do you monitor security issues?

5.   Do you have an information classification structure designed to identify and protect valuable information in your company?

6.   User training is an essential component of information security management. How do you train your staff?

7.   What levels of access control would be of most value to your business?

8.   Do you have business continuity plans, and how often do you test them?

9.   How often do you review your information security management procedures?

10.   Does your Chief Executive know how a security breach will be handled?

If you are not able to provide complete answers to each of these questions then ISO 17799 will help you to improve your corporate information security management.

Section 2
E-commerce and Information Security Management

The popular use of the term 'e-commerce' suggests that there is something new or special about the information being passed between vendor and buyer just because it is done electronically, rather than over the table in a face-to-face meeting. It is our contention that this information is just the same as it ever was. A contract in English Law, and in most other legal systems around the world, is still essentially an offer, an acceptance and a consideration. The magic component that e-commerce adds is to enable that contract process to happen in so-called 'cyberspace'.

E-businesses, or 'dot-com' companies, are often merely brokers managing websites, which themselves are little more than advertising hoardings for their selected product. The dot-com company acts as an information broker, much as, for example, catalogue sales companies have done for many years. A major difference is that the actual value or size of the dot-com company is potentially masked by the simple fact that no one ever sees its assets face to face. Consider then the three essential components to any contract.

THE OFFER

The popular press is full of anecdotes relating how teenage computer wizards are able to establish international businesses from their bedrooms merely by launching a website that outsells the efforts of major companies with the product of their choice. For most websites the expertise of the graphic designer is what sells the product.

So what is different? What has changed from visual advertisements on cinema or television?

The main difference is the cost and accessibility of the media required to generate an eye-catching website. Previously, a 'Pearl & Dean' advertisement at the local cinema, perhaps advertising a curry house conveniently placed within a few steps of the cinema, was only screened locally and was easily verified by a quick glimpse into the curry house window on the way home. A television advertisement might reach a nation-wide audience but would cost a considerable amount of money, and therefore probably represent a successful national branded product.

By contrast, the teenage bedroom website can appear as professional as any other, it can reach a worldwide distribution and no one will ever know the difference between that and a similar website operated by a genuine blue chip company.

THE ACCEPTANCE

'Click on Buy' almost says it all.

A significant component of e-commerce is the ease with which the potential buyer is able to make that critical buying decision. 'Click on Buy', and await the acceptance of your order by the vendor, often by instant e-mail reply. There can be few people in business or in their private lives who would not admit to over-ordering from a catalogue merely because they are doing it in the privacy of their own office or living room.

THE CONSIDERATION

How should you pay for goods in the e-commerce marketplace?

Electronic funds transfer is now such an old-fashioned expression that it is hardly ever mentioned in polite circles. To move funds from one account to another is so easy that it can be done at the click of the mouse from office or home. Paying a phone bill on-line is as easy as paying for a large commercial order of goods to be shipped half way around the world.

So where's the danger?

E-COMMERCE SECURITY

The essential components of good security have not changed. *Confidentiality*, *integrity* and *availability* are still the key elements of strong security. What has changed is the ability to evidence those criteria, especially in cases where the organisation which owns the information in question is visible only as a website on a server, managed by a third party in an undisclosed location.

CONFIDENTIALITY

Who has access to your information?

Once your corporate data is on the web it is theoretically available to the proverbial world and his wife. Perhaps that is what you intended. On the other hand, perhaps you did not intend for your costs to be as public as your price list. Once your information is published on a world-wide scale, you will have less control over your ability to arrange special deals for special customers.

INTEGRITY

Who can modify your information?

Hacking is a real threat to any online and available information system. Hacking, or more properly 'computer misuse', is an offence in law and liable to be punished accordingly; however, that could all be far too late once the damage has been done. Experience shows that companies suffer more from internal computer misuse than ever they do from malicious hackers. In most cases this misuse is due to poor training and inadequate system protection; an elaborate way of describing 'finger trouble'. Sometimes this misuse is deliberate on the part of a disgruntled employee, or outright cheating of the system.

The only complete answer to the issue of information integrity is to have strong control over information access. It is worth noting that in this context information is not just that held in digital form on your computer systems. Password control over terminal and network access is fine so long as it is matched by a similar degree of protection over the printed, hard copy left in the in-tray for any passer-by to see.

AVAILABILITY

Who needs to know, and how well can you control external access?

It is fairly simple to envisage ways to control access to paper files through a conventional document registry system. It is less easy to control access when you are part of a world-wide publishing system like your Internet website. It is of course possible to give selected clients a suitable password that will allow them access to a private room on your website, where they can read selected and specially focused information. But then how well will they protect your password?

E-COMMERCE SECURITY AS A TWO-WAY STREET

It is clear that any company wishing to protect its information should adopt the established route, starting with a risk analysis to determine what is of value to the company and how best to protect it. It is equally clear that the tools and techniques put in place to provide a secure environment must be audited and maintained if they are to continue to provide corporate value once the initial investment has been made. ISO 17799 as a management standard, provides an excellent set of guidelines and principles to adopt as a control over the subject and allows a company to measure its performance against a set of internationally recognised criteria.

But, e-commerce security is a more complex issue.

The fundamental premise of e-commerce is that corporate information, your corporate information, is shared as freely as possible with your trading partners.

Can you establish how well your trading partners manage the security of your information once it has been so freely shared?

Where does your confidential corporate information actually go once you have electronically submitted your best and final price on that 'make or break' tender?

The real answer is that you will never actually know where it has gone once it has left your office. The only way you can improve the levels of confidence that it has been best managed along the way is to look for similar levels of good management practice in the company that carries the information and in the company that you are trading with. And if you agree with that statement, then you must believe that they will be looking for that degree of confidence from you.

ISO 17799 is a certification standard that can be independently audited. The independent audit is critical to that public confidence factor in the open information marketplace.

ISO 17799 has the potential to create huge market advantage for those companies that offer to host information or act as intermediaries in the electronic market.

SO WHAT WILL IT ALL COST?

As always there is a range of answers to such a question. ISO17799 is a management standard and this guide is about how best to manage the topic. Management policies and practices cost very little to develop; the real cost rests with the choice of security tools and services that you choose to implement. Use the risk assessment as the basis for the business case to justify subsequent expenditure on the tools. Use your common sense to decide how important it will be to your business to ensure that you manage information security in a cost-effective way.

ISO17799 INFORMATION SECURITY MANAGEMENT

The following sections of this guide are based on the ten sections of ISO17799. In each section the top-level objectives are paraphrased from the standard and the accompanying commentary is designed to explore the rationale behind their inclusion.

The ten sections of ISO17799 are:

Section 1.   Security policy

Section 2.   Organisational security

Section 3.   Asset classification and control

Section 4.   Personnel security

Section 5.   Physical and environmental security

Section 6.   Computer and operations management

Section 7.   Access control

Section 8.   Systems development and maintenance

Section 9.   Business continuity management

Section 10.   Compliance

Section 3
Security Policy

INFORMATION SECURITY POLICY

Objective: to provide management direction and support for information security.

Top management should set a clear direction and demonstrate their support for and commitment to information security through the issue of a security policy across the organisation.

- A written policy document should be approved by management, be published, and communicated to all employees responsible for information security. This should be done in a manner that is understandable to those employees.

- The owner of the policy document must ensure that the policy is reviewed according to a pre-determined schedule.

COMMENTARY

Corporate management is always a complex mixture of interpretation and implementation. In a small organisation it is possible for managers to rely on their close contact with their employees to pass their intentions around the workforce. In larger organisations or in those where external regulators or auditors require it, there is a need for management intentions to be published in the form of documented corporate policies. In general these policy statements serve a number of valuable purposes.

1.   The primary object of a policy statement is to outline the aims of the company as endorsed by the executive management team.

2.   The document should be written in a way that can be interpreted at a local level into the operational rules or Standard Operating Procedures.

3.   The rules which are then derived from the overall policy statement will control the day-by-day operations that occur at the various functional levels within the company. It is unrealistic to expect the corporate executive to write those detailed rules.

4.   The existence of a policy statement, endorsed by the executive, implies that it will be recognised as a valid budget item and funded accordingly.

5.   The policy document is also the means by which you tell your staff what the rules are. Remember that unless you do tell them, there is no way you can ensure that they stick to them.

SECURITY POLICY CHECKLIST

As a general guideline the information security policy statement should include:

- A definition of information security, with objectives and the scope of the topic as seen by the corporate management team.

- A statement of management's commitment to the implementation of the aims of the policy.

- A rationale for spending time and effort on establishing security: how and why it is seen as being important to the company and its future.

- An explanation of the need for specific aspects of the policy, such as virus controls or the need to comply with specific legislation.

- The allocation of responsibilities for the continued implementation of the policy.

- An explanation of the process for reporting breaches of security.

It is inevitable that any policy or given set of rules will sooner or later be found wanting.

The intention to review these corporate requirements, as an executive function and from the top down, must be conveyed in the policy statement. Many companies leave this review process in the hands of their audit department. The expression 'audit and review' can be misleading in that it suggests that these two important functions can be combined. The review process can easily become entangled with the audit function, but it is important to remember that auditors are employed to check compliance with the rules; they are not strictly speaking supposed to make the rules which they audit . This poacher and gamekeeper approach is inevitably doomed to fail.

Experience shows that if employees are failing to adhere to the rules, it is often because the rules are poorly written, or no longer apply because the company business has changed in some way. The issue of employees' access rights and permission levels is especially vulnerable to these gradual, evolutionary changes in working practices.

It is essential that the rules are owned and set by the corporate management chain and not by the auditors. Auditors may be required to advise the management as to the statutory, regulatory and legal implications of any given working procedures, but only the company management should be allowed to publish the rules as to how those procedures are carried out.

In most companies, only the corporate executive team can legitimately change the company policy. It seems unlikely that any Board of Directors would allow their internal or external auditors to determine their company policies, so why let them make the rules by which those policies are delivered?

Section 4
Security Organisation

INFORMATION SECURITY INFRASTRUCTURE

Objective: to manage information security within the organisation.

- A management framework should be established to initiate and control the implementation of information security within the organisation.

- Management direction should be provided through a suitable high-level steering forum.

- In a large organisation it might be necessary to co-ordinate information security measures through a cross-functional forum.

- Responsibilities for the protection of individual assets and for carrying out specific security processes should be explicitly defined.

- Installation of IT facilities should be technically approved and authorised.

- Specialist advice on information security may be required.

- Security specialists and organisations should co-operate to combat general security threats.

- Implementation of information security should be independently reviewed.

SECURITY OF THIRD-PARTY ACCESS

Objective: to maintain the security of organisational IT facilities and of access to information assets by third parties.

Access to company IT facilities by (non-organisational) third parties should be controlled.

- The risks associated with access to organisational IT facilities by third parties should be assessed, and appropriate security controls implemented.

- Contracts with third parties involving access to organisational IT facilities should specify security conditions.

OUTSOURCING

Objective: to maintain the security of information when the responsibility for information processing has been outsourced to another organisation.

Outsourcing arrangements must address in the contract all security measures, procedures, reporting and management structures to ensure that the outsourcer applies appropriate security.

- The contract with the outsourcing supplier should address all security responsibilities, logical and physical security to be applied, business continuity management and the right audit.

COMMENTARY

It is important to ensure that the corporate organisation is positive about its delegation of security responsibility to areas where those responsibilities can be properly discharged. To be fair, we do not see many companies prepared to appoint a security officer at Board level but we do believe that the topic should be on the Board meeting agenda because that is where the buck will stop if or when it all goes wrong. The security profession is most often split between the general administration office, where the topic usually centres on physical security through the use of uniformed guards and CCTV cameras, and the IT security office, primarily concerned with firewalls, encryption and password protection. Consequently the Board-level representation is often split, and only occasionally is that split ever successfully healed.

When companies delegate physical security to the Administration Director and computer security to the IT Director, this splits the job and the budget such that neither Director can deliver the best security value for money to the company. This situation should be avoided wherever possible. As companies move into e-commerce the need for a strong image of corporate information security is seen to be paramount.

It is stressed that this section is primarily about people rather than technology, and about how they are organised to manage the security of information in their departments. As with most business processes this is a multi-level activity. At the executive level, the corporate security policy will outline the broad objectives, while the subordinate management levels will interpret that policy into specific rules. The resultant mix can often require a compromise where there are practical limits on the degree of control and auditing which can be achieved within the operational function. This could well result in similar policies being met in differing ways by different parts of the organisation, with sets of rules each designed to fit best with the local working conditions.

The key messages are to allocate responsibility positively and then to empower those staff by giving them proper authorisation to discharge their responsibilities. This enabling process often involves the use of specialist forums or steering groups as the guardians of the interpretation of corporate policy across the organisation.

Companies with limited resources should consider retaining external specialist advice, especially where they anticipate the need for investigation into security breaches that might eventually lead to disciplinary action.

This delegation of responsibility requires regular review as the business grows and is especially important with regard to external organisations and other companies with whom you are trading. The more remote the third party the more the need to arrange formal ways to review the implementation of security management between parties.

The concept of 'back-to-back' contract terms and conditions is not new. If you enter into a contract which requires a nominated degree of security management from your company, you had better make sure that your suppliers are not going to let you down.

Section 5
Assets, Classification and Control

ACCOUNTABILITY FOR ASSETS

Objective: to maintain appropriate protection of organisational assets.

All major information assets should be accounted for and have a nominated owner.

- Inventories should be maintained of all assets.

INFORMATION CLASSIFICATION

Objective: to ensure that information assets receive an appropriate level of protection.

Security classifications should be used to indicate the need and priorities for security protection.

- Protection for classified information should be consistent with business needs. Classifications should show the value, sensitivity and criticality of the asset.

- Classified information and outputs from systems handling organisationally classified data should be labelled appropriately.

COMMENTARY

Legend has it that a bank robber was once asked why he robbed banks. His answer was: 'Because that's where the money is.'

A successful business is usually one that has good control over the management of its resources. To achieve that control it is critical to understand 'where the money is'. If you do not know which assets are important to the company and which are less so, and where they are at any time, then how can you protect the good bits? Remember that in today's world of inexpensive hardware, the information on your systems will almost always be worth more than the box that contains it.

The previous section identifies the need for delegated security responsibility. The managers who accept that delegation need to know precisely what is of value to the company and the degree to which it must be kept secure. Without such definition it is impossible to meet those security responsibilities. This section is designed to assist managers to decide just what is important to the company by creating a formal scheme against which all working information can be classified.

The military environment has for years used what is primarily a three-layer security classification scheme to determine confidentiality. The three layers are:

Unrestricted; Restricted; and Secret.

Unrestricted information, in any medium is freely distributed, with no need for special handling routines. Restricted material should only be passed around under cover of closed envelopes. Secret material is passed in sealed envelopes and is signed for by a suitable authorised party at each point where it changes hands.

Experience shows that in the majority of companies the information that qualifies for Secret treatment is regularly less than ten per cent of all communications. Restricted information is usually between 15 per cent and 20 per cent of all communications. The balance is Unrestricted and not worth expending special resources on.

However, it is important to note that the growth of e-commerce and dot-com companies will change that conventional balance. The companies in this field are essentially purveyors of information, and if information is your product then it could be that your higher levels of security should extend to almost everything you do.

The desk-top IT environment is particularly prone to 'organic' growth, where comparatively inexpensive items of equipment and software become host to critical business processes without necessarily attracting the corresponding degree of protection.

It is only possible to protect your high value assets if you know what and where they are!

Given delegated responsibility for corporate policy down through all departments of the managerial chain, this section is about the need for managers to identify where those controls should be applied.

Just as only the corporate executive can legitimately own the corporate policy, so only the line managers can know which are the important files, where they are kept and which individual employees need access to them in order to work effectively.

A word of warning!

It is always tempting for individuals to over-classify work, in the genuine belief that the work they do is important. Important does not always equal secret. The better the definition of what should and should not be deemed classified, the more effectively the system will operate.

Section 6
Personnel Security

SECURITY IN JOB DEFINITION AND RESOURCING

Objective: to reduce the risks of human error, theft, fraud, or misuse of facilities.

Security should be addressed at the recruitment stage, included in the job descriptions and contracts, and monitored during the individual's employment.

- Job descriptions should define security roles and responsibilities.

- Applications for employment should be screened if the job involves access to an organisation's IT facilities or handling secure information.

- Users of organisational IT facilities should sign a confidentiality undertaking.

USER TRAINING

Objective: to ensure that users are aware of information security threats and concerns, and are equipped to support organisational security policy in the course of their normal work.

Users should be trained in security procedures and the correct use of IT facilities.

- Users should be given adequate security education and technical training.

RESPONDING TO INCIDENTS

Objective: to minimise the damage from security incidents and malfunctions and to monitor and learn from such incidents.

Incidents affecting security should be reported through management channels as quickly as possible.

- Suspected security weaknesses should be reported.

- Software malfunctions should be reported

- A disciplinary process is essential for dealing with security breaches.

COMMENTARY

It is worth noting that this section contains two of the most significant control features of the standard: the education and training of staff, and a formal, published route for reporting breaches of security.

The old canon that ignorance of the rules is no excuse is all very well as a directive for the prosecution of offenders at the subsequent board of enquiry. However, it would have been much better for all concerned if the event had never occurred.

Having published your company security policy in Step 1 and set out the organisation in Step 2, the next stage is to train the staff in the detail of how the company expects those instructions to be carried out.

The start point, and the missing factor in most organisations, is the need to recognise the responsibility for security in the initial job description. If you intend to operate a secure environment, the need for your employees to appreciate what that implies becomes paramount. If they understand this on the day they join your company so much the better. As with all commercial skills there will be some degree of trade-off when you recruit new staff. It is rare to find the perfect fit in any category, but the recruitment process should give the company a good idea of the subsequent training targets for each individual. If the company expects to handle secret information, then the employee's contract should include a non-disclosure agreement, and you should make sure that he or she understands what that means.

A well-managed organisation is the one where things do not go wrong, rather than the one where all the guilty are duly punished. Regular security training for all staff who have security responsibility is the only way to help them achieve the company's objectives. There are many companies where induction training is only done once per year. Anyone who joined in the last year could have spent a long time doing things which left you vulnerable simply because no one told them otherwise. If the company is large enough to experience a high volume of new starters then it would be better to arrange induction training at more frequent intervals. If you have very few new starters, it may be worth considering appointing individual mentors who are charged with passing on the good word.

'Out-sourcing', 'down-sizing' and 'de-layering' are popular terms for reducing the corporate headcount. Whichever flavour you recognise, you will probably also recognise the increase in the use of third-party contractors who come and go in order to fill the gaps.

Who bothers to spend valuable contractor time on induction training?

Temporary staff, who come and go from an agency without you even knowing their home address, must be considered as the worst possible risk to your security systems. Either train them and supervise them, or don't let them near your secure information!

Sadly, it is not a perfect world, and when breaches of security do occur, for whatever reason, it is important to contain the result by reporting the incident and responding to it as quickly as possible.

Who should you report such an incident to?

What information about the incident will that person need to know?

What immediate precautions should you take to limit the company's exposure to the security breach?

It may be that there will be little or no time to organise a response to the incident, in which case the more thinking which has gone into the response procedure the better off you will be.

Remember that if the response is likely to include formal disciplinary action then the full process should be formally described and approved by the company management to remove the possibility of dispute after the event.

Section 7
Physical and Environmental Security

SECURE AREAS

Objective: to prevent unauthorised access, damage and interference to IT services.

IT facilities supporting critical or sensitive business activities should be housed in secure areas.

- Physical security protection should be based on defined perimeters.

- Secure areas should be protected by appropriate entry controls.

- Data centres and computer rooms supporting critical business activities should have good physical security.

- An intermediate holding area should be considered for deliveries to computer rooms.

- A clear-desk policy should protect information from unauthorised access and loss or damage.

- Removal of property belonging to the organisation should require authorisation.

EQUIPMENT SECURITY

Objective: to prevent loss, damage or compromise of assets and interruption to business activities.

Equipment should be physically protected from security threats and environmental hazards.

- Equipment should be so sited or protected as to reduce the risk of damage, interference or unauthorised access.

- Equipment should be protected from power supply failures or other electrical anomalies.

- Power and telecommunication cables should be protected from interception or damage.

- Equipment should be properly maintained.

- Security procedures and controls should cover the security of equipment used outside an organisation's premises.

- Data should be erased from equipment prior to disposal.

COMMENTARY

Physical security is a familiar area, with its attendant locks and passes and uniformed guards. Most companies will have placed much of this responsibility in the hands of professional security officers, who are practised at monitoring physical and often therefore visible security measures. Information security is usually far less visible, and often relies on technology that is outside the experience of the physical security experts.

With the policy and the organisation and training in place, this section reviews the overlap between the familiar physical, visible security and the far less visible security of information. This standard assumes that most of a company's information will reside within its computer systems. Information security management is therefore heavily dependent on keeping safe the hardware infrastructure which hosts that information.

In the days of mainframe machines that weighed tons and were connected to chilled water and complex three-phase power supplies, the theft of whole computers was almost inconceivable, and yet almost every computer hall was protected by card locks and halon gas. Today we have our critical corporate information on computers on our desks, in open-plan office environments, and we rarely bother to lock anything away when we leave the office.

Technology seems to work against us in that the trends are towards ever more portable versions of machines, which allow both the information and the means to process it to be carried easily between home and office, with no loss of working capacity. The theft of portable laptop machines is on the increase. They can be replaced, but the information on them is often the only copy.

Imagine leaving your laptop on the train in the morning, especially when you worked until midnight to finish that critical report...

The significance of this section is that it raises the profile of computing assets to a more appropriate level on the corporate physical security agenda. Individual PCs might only be worth a modest amount when new, and even less after depreciation on the asset register, but they often contain your vital information up to the very end of their useful life. Indeed, many PCs leave the company on retirement to the scrap heap with hard disks full of corporate spreadsheets and letters to the Chairman!

Section 8
Computer and Network Management

OPERATIONAL PROCEDURES AND RESPONSIBILITIES

Objective: to ensure the correct and secure operation of computer and network facilities.

Responsibilities and procedures for the management of all computers and networks should be established.

- The operating procedures identified by the information security policy should be documented and maintained under formal change control.

- Incident management responsibilities and procedures, including escalation procedures, should be established.

- Segregation of duties minimises the risk of negligent or deliberate system misuse.

- Development and testing facilities should be isolated from operational systems.

- Proposals to use external facilities management services should identify the full security implications and include appropriate security controls.

SYSTEM PLANNING AND ACCEPTANCE

Objective: to minimise the risk of system failure.

Advance planning and preparation are required to ensure the availability of adequate capacity and resources.

- Capacity requirements should be monitored to avoid failures due to inadequate capacity and/or system bottlenecks.

- Acceptance criteria for new systems should be established and suitable tests carried out prior to acceptance.

- Fallback planning should be co-ordinated and reviewed.

- Changes to IT facilities and systems should be controlled.

PROTECTION FROM MALICIOUS SOFTWARE

Objective: to safeguard the integrity of software and data.

Precautions are required to prevent and detect the introduction of malicious software.

- Virus detection and protection measures, appropriate procedures, and user awareness and training should be implemented.

HOUSEKEEPING

Objective: to maintain the integrity and availability of IT services.

Housekeeping measures are required to maintain the integrity and availability of services.

- Back-up copies of essential business data and software should be regularly taken.

- Computer operators should maintain a log of all work carried out.

- Faults should be reported and corrective action taken.

- Computer environments should be monitored where necessary.

NETWORK MANAGEMENT

Objective: to ensure the safeguarding of information in networks and the protection of the supporting infrastructure.

The security management of computer networks, which may span organisational boundaries, requires special attention.

- A range of security controls is required in computer networks. The detailed requirement will vary with the network vendor and with the service level implemented

MEDIA HANDLING

Objective: to prevent damage to assets and interruptions to business activities.

Computer media should be controlled and physically protected.

- Removable computer media should be controlled.

- Procedures for handling sensitive data should be established.

- System documentation should be protected from unauthorised access.

- Computer media should be disposed of securely and safely when no longer required.

DATA AND SOFTWARE EXCHANGE

Objective: to prevent the loss, modification or misuse of data.

Exchanges of data and software between organisations should be controlled.

- Agreements for the exchange of data and software should specify security controls.

- Computer media in transit should be protected from loss or misuse.

- Special security controls should be applied where necessary, to protect electronic data interchange.

- Controls should be applied where necessary, to reduce the business and security risks associated with electronic mail.

- Clear policies and guidelines are required to control the business and security risks associated with electronic office systems.

NB: The Data Protection Act requires some specific controls to ensure that EU controls are not compromised when data is moved outside the EU zone.

COMMENTARY

This is one of the largest sections in the standard, and reflects the importance of security in the electronic environment through good management of the computers and network by those members of the IT department who are responsible for the task.

Most large organisations who are able to support professional IT departments will find that their own IT management procedures address the topics raised in this section, and probably much more. The importance of this section is that it brings together the need for these professional IT management procedures with good professional business management procedures. Often the IT department is operated at a staff level that enables it to provide the service required by the business users, but does not allow for the management overhead to run their own offices in a professional manner. Often the only interface between the IT department and the business users is the overworked help desk, where the staff spend all day resolving queries of one sort or another. It is important to recognise the changes brought about by what is now a well-established client-server environment in the workplace. Business users are often equally as IT-aware as their professional counterparts, and very capable of creating additional copies of critical files or e-mailing documents home for use at another time.

Many organisations that depend on large client-server networks manage their inventory with little or no on-site professional IT management. The reliability and replacement costs of the current generation of equipment mean that often companies feel able to dispense with on-site maintenance engineers. The controls identified in this section are no less important to those companies and must, if necessary, be implemented by non-IT managers.

The first section in this chapter—operational procedures and responsibilities—is especially important. Once again this emphasis on documented procedures underpins the ability to determine what is required at all levels of the business, how it should be done and who should do it.

A large number of companies have elected to allow free access to the company systems for Internet and associated e-mail services. The primary control over this personal traffic will be the 'firewall' system, but it is important to recognise that very few firewalls will be programmed to censor the content of personal e-mail. There has been a growing number of recent examples where poor discretion in the use of company e-mail services could well lead to the loss of reputation for the company. If employees are not formally warned about such behaviour it will be difficult to take any formal action to prevent it recurring.

The text of each section and sub-section of the standard is brief and deliberately left open to interpretation, for use by large and small companies alike. It is worth remembering that ISO17799 is designed to provide a checklist for managers and that it does not purport to be a complete operations manual. Used as a checklist this section will prompt the right questions of those professionals either inside or outside the company.

Section 9
System Access
Control

BUSINESS REQUIREMENTS FOR SYSTEM ACCESS

Objective: to control access to business information.

Access to computer services and data should be controlled on the basis of business requirements.

- Business requirements for access control should be defined according to the specific user requirements and documented for reference by the System Administrator.

USER ACCESS MANAGEMENT

Objective: to prevent unauthorised computer access.

There should be formal procedures to control allocation of access rights to IT services.

- There should be a formal user registration and de-registration procedure for access to all multi-user IT services.

- The use of special privileges should be restricted and controlled.

- The allocation of user passwords should be securely controlled.

- User access rights should be reviewed at regular intervals.

USER RESPONSIBILITIES

Objective: to prevent unauthorised user access.

The co-operation of authorised users is essential for effective security.

- Users should follow good security practices in the selection and use of passwords.

- Users should ensure that unattended equipment has appropriate security protection.

NETWORK ACCESS CONTROL

Objective: to protect network services.

Connections to networked services should be controlled.

- Users should only be able to gain access to the services that they are authorised to use.

- The route from the user terminal to the computer service may need to be controlled.

- Connections by remote users via public (or non-organisational) networks should be authenticated.

- Connections by remote computer systems should be authenticated.

- Access to diagnostic ports should be securely controlled.

- Large networks may require to be divided into separate domains.

- The connection capability of users may need to be controlled, to support the access control policy requirements of certain business applications.

- Shared networks may require network routing controls.

- The risks associated with the use of network services should be established.

COMPUTER ACCESS CONTROL

Objective: to prevent unauthorised computer access.

Access to computer facilities should be controlled.

- Automatic terminal identification should be considered to authenticate connections to specific locations.

- Access to IT services should be via a secure log-on process.

- Computer activities should be traceable to individuals.

- An effective password system should be used to authenticate users.

- Provision of duress alarms should be considered for users who might be the target of coercion.

- Inactive terminals in high-risk locations, or servicing high-risk systems, should be set to time out, to prevent access by unauthorised persons.

- Restrictions of connection times should provide additional security for high-risk applications.

APPLICATION ACCESS CONTROL

Objective: to prevent unauthorised access to information held in computer systems.

Logical access controls should be used to control access to application systems and data.

- Access to data and IT services should be granted in accordance with business access policy.

- Access to system utilities should be restricted and controlled.

- Access to program source libraries should be restricted and controlled.

- Sensitive systems might require a dedicated (isolated) computing environment.

MONITORING SYSTEM ACCESS AND USE

Objective: to detect unauthorised activities.

Systems should be monitored to ensure conformity to access policy and standards.

- Audit trails of security events should be maintained.

- Procedures for monitoring system use should be established.

- Computer clocks should be synchronised for accurate recording.

COMMENTARY

The previous sections have dealt with corporate policy and organisation for identifying that which should be protected and that which is less important, and with the tools and procedures necessary to enable corporate information to be managed in a secure fashion. This section is about who is authorised to have access to corporate information.

System access can be controlled in a number of ways, using hardware or software. The real question is not how the control is achieved but who is allowed access and to what. System access is like every other system of locks and keys which can be either logical or physical or both. The basic decisions are what requires protection and who has the keys. These are strictly business decisions, which the technology should exist to service.

The decision-making process is a simple two-stage affair. First, nominate those business applications that should be protected, e.g. finance/budgets. Second, nominate who requires access to that application, e.g. the Finance Director and give him or her the keys to allocate wisely to his or her staff, taking care not to give everyone, including the office temp, the keys to the crown jewels!

The military have an expression 'Need to Know'. The term implies that only those who need to know any given information in order to do their job should be authorised to have access to that information. This is not to confuse secrecy with security, nor is it to suggest that those outside the sphere of interest are not also interested.

Information will often change its classification over its life span. Next year's prices might be top-secret information until they are announced, and then everyone knows. Taking the above example—perhaps the spread sheets being used in the Finance Department to plan next year's budgets—it seems obvious that only those who are directly involved in the planning exercise should be authorised to access those figures until they are ready to be published. When the final figures are approved they might be moved to a read-only file, so that the information can be put on a wider circulation. Access control is about making information available to the right people in a secure way, which means that other people cannot alter that information without proper authority.

The decisions regarding who are the right people are business decisions, not IT decisions. The IT department can provide the tools by way of passwords, encryption, secure routing and log-on procedures, but only the business managers can decide whom those controls will apply to.

In practical terms the locks and keys are either hardware or software and, just as with any other type of locks, there are varying qualities to be had. The most common type of lock is either the user identity or password that must be keyed in to allow entry to the system. The technicians can install these password system but only the business managers can ensure that individual users use them sensibly, i.e. use obscure passwords rather than their own name, change their password frequently and do not leave the password written on a post-it note stuck to the side of the screen.

If the information that you need to protect is really important, the hardware solutions are usually better than software. Fit key-card locks and issue magnetic swipe cards to those people authorised to switch the machine on. For the most important information, keep it off the network on a stand-alone machine and lock it up in a separate room. Even the smartest hackers can only steal information from machines that are switched on and connected to the outside world.

Section 10
Systems Development and Maintenance

SECURITY REQUIREMENTS OF SYSTEMS

Objective: to ensure that security is built into IT systems.

Security requirements should be identified and agreed prior to the development of IT systems.

- An analysis of security requirements should be carried out and specified by the business unit sponsor at the requirements analysis stage of each development project.

SECURITY IN APPLICATION SYSTEMS

Objective: to prevent loss, modification or misuse of user data in application systems.

Appropriate security controls, including audit trails, should be designed into application systems.

- Data input into application systems should be validated.

- Data processed by application systems should be validated.

- Encryption should be considered for highly sensitive data.

- A message authentication system should be considered for applications that involve the transmission of sensitive data.

CRYPTOGRAPHIC CONTROLS

Objective: to protect the confidentiality, authenticity or integrity of information

Cryptographic systems and techniques should be used for the protection of information that is considered at risk and for which other controls do not provide adequate protection.

- An organisation should develop a policy on the use of cryptographic controls for the protection of its information.

- Encryption should be considered for protecting critical or sensitive information.

SECURITY OF SYSTEM FILES

Objective: to ensure that IT project and support activities are conducted in a secure manner.

Access to system files should be controlled.

- Strict control should be exercised over the implementation of software on operational systems.

- Test data should be protected and controlled.

SECURITY IN DEVELOPMENT AND SUPPORT ENVIRONMENTS

Objective: to maintain the security of application systems software and data.

Project and support environments should be strictly controlled.

- Formal change control procedures should be enforced.

- The impact of operating system changes should be reviewed and tested to ensure that there is no adverse impact on security.

- Modifications to software packages should be discouraged. Any essential changes should be strictly controlled.

- Where covert channels or Trojan code are a concern the software should be thoroughly inspected and tested before release into the production environment.

- Where software development is outsourced it should be closely monitored, fully tested and subject to an appropriate contract.

COMMENTARY

It is essential that those companies who are able to commission or design their own systems and applications take every opportunity to make those systems fail-safe by the use of in-built controls. As with Section 6, this section is intended primarily as a guide to the technical team and for the advice of smaller companies who do not undertake their own development programmes. Companies who maintain such software development teams will doubtless be aware of the controls required to safeguard their final production systems.

The physical separation between versions of software under development and those 'frozen' and released into the change control process is an essential aspect of good system control.

Developers are often obliged to use extreme cases of input data in order to test the limits of their software. The overlap between these environments where 'test' information can suddenly become 'real' is known to be the source of many computer frauds, e.g. the junior software program writer who gives himself the Managing Director's authority to approve expenses 'just to test the system', or as happened to a major UK bank, the head of an overseas office develops (created) an unauthorised account in which to bury his trading losses.

Encryption is the technique of mathematically altering the binary code in the computer to produce a number that can only be unscrambled by reversing the mathematics. The problem with mathematics is that it just happens to be the subject which computers are especially good at, and determined hackers are often able to break the code. Encryption algorithms are only better than passwords if they are very complex and therefore often correspondingly expensive. However, if your assets are that important to your company then encryption may be worth the cost.

It is essential to review the levels of protection that are incorporated into the operating systems on a regular basis. It is not uncommon for the value of a particular part of the company to change over the years and for the locks on the doors to be forgotten.

It is also worth considering that even smaller companies do sometimes commission software developers to build customised software for them. When third parties are involved, it is even more important to be sure that the software which you have commissioned has been cleaned up before it is released into the production environment. The fact that the rogue junior programmer is not actually an employee of yours may just serve to compound the problem if the worst comes to the worst.

As a general rule, if your company is not large enough to support an in-house software development team you will probably be better off sticking with proprietary software in its shrink-wrapped form and resisting the urge to modify it, beyond incorporating your own company logo into the package.

Section 11
Business Continuity Planning

ASPECTS OF BUSINESS CONTINUITY PLANNING

Objective: to counteract interruptions to business activities and to protect critical business processes from the effects of major failures or disasters.

A business continuity management process should be implemented to reduce the disruption caused by disasters and security failures to an acceptable level, through a combination of preventative and recovery controls.

- There should be a managed process in place for developing and maintaining business continuity throughout the organisation.

- Owners of business resources and processes should identify the impacts of a number of events that could cause interruptions to their business processes, and a strategy should be developed to determine the overall approach to business continuity.

- Plans should be developed to maintain or restore business operations, in the required time scales identified by the business, following an interruption to, or failure of, critical services.

- A single framework of business continuity plans should be maintained to ensure that all departments are consistent.

- Business continuity plans should be regularly tested and maintained.

COMMENTARY

Business continuity planning is an essential component in all aspects of business. There can be few purchasing departments who do not have lists of 'second source' suppliers who can step in should their first choice let them down. There can be few transport departments who do not have a plan to cover vehicle breakdowns or absentee drivers. Why should the administration office not have similar plans for how it intends to deliver corporate information when the power goes off, or when the computers break down?

The IT department may be required to play a major role in replacing lost or damaged systems and infrastructure, but the main thrust must come from the business managers, who are the only ones who can decide what parts of their business they need to carry on doing and just how much equipment they need to support their line function to a satisfactory degree. Invariably there are two key criticalities when disaster strikes: those things which must be completed within the next few hours, and those things where the volume of transactions is such that the backlog of work will rapidly become unmanageable if it is not controlled. Only the business managers will know how badly they are affected by the specific incident on the day that it happens.

It has already been stressed that compliance with this standard will have special significance for those companies with whom your company may wish to network. All partners in such trading networks need to share a known level of confidence about the security of information passing around the network. It is equally important that the partners can rely on each other to be there when this information is being passed around. Once electronic trading partners get to 'know' each other it is not uncommon for shared processes to build up over the network, e.g. Company A cannot complete its monthly sales return until Company B downloads its component of the spreadsheet, and so on.

Business continuity planning can be as important to your trading partners as it is to your customers and to your own survivability. There is growing evidence of major contracts including business continuity management as a mandatory requirement in the tendering process.

Section 12
Compliance

COMPLIANCE WITH LEGAL REQUIREMENTS

Objective: to avoid breaches of any criminal or civil law, of statutory, regulatory or contractual obligations and of any security requirements.

The design, operation and use of information systems may be subject to statutory and contractual security requirements.

- All relevant statutory, regulatory and contractual requirements should be explicitly defined and documented.

- Appropriate controls should be implemented to ensure compliance with the relevant legal requirements for the use of copyright or trademarked material.

- Important records of an organisation should be protected from loss, destruction and falsification.

- Applications handling personal data on individuals should comply with the relevant data protection legislation and principles.

- Information processing facilities should only be used for authorised business purposes.

- Legislation regarding encryption in all countries where organisational data or information processing facilities may reside must be understood and obeyed.

- Evidence used in either civil or criminal action must conform to the relevant rules for presentation of evidence for the jurisdiction in which the action is being brought.

REVIEWS OF SECURITY POLICY AND TECHNICAL COMPLIANCE

Objective: to ensure compliance of systems with organisational security policies and standards.

The security of IT systems should be regularly reviewed.

- All areas within the organisation should be considered for regular review to ensure compliance with security policies and standards.

- IT facilities should be regularly checked for compliance with security implementation standards.

SYSTEM AUDIT CONSIDERATIONS

Objective: to maximise the effectiveness of and to minimise interference to/from the system audit process

There should be controls to safeguard operational systems and audit tools during system audits.

- Audits of operational systems should be planned and agreed.

- Access to system audit tools should be controlled.

COMMENTARY

It is clear that the authors of this standard place great emphasis on compliance. Two of the four mandatory controls are found within this section.

As a final comment on the final section of the standard it is most important to appreciate this document as being a management standard. The text is designed to allow the rules to be written to meet all sizes and types of company. The layout of the standard is intended to steer the reader through the subject in the most appropriate order by stating the corporate objectives in the initial policy document and then exploring the ways and means to achieve those objectives. All that effort could be wasted if there was no way of checking that the working procedures were actually delivering the goods.

'Compliance', 'audit', 'review', are all terms which address that process of checking whether things are working as expected. In most companies, new products, new customers and new trading conditions will be a constant source of change, which will cause these security controls to become stale. If the controls are not working, then it may well be that the business has changed as well as the people failing to get it right.

How will you know if you don't check?